TORBAY

THE VISIBLE HISTORY

JACK WHITTON

BOSSINEY BOOKS · LAUNCESTON

Fortifications on Berry Head, erected during the Napoleonic wars (1793-1815) to prevent the French landing in Tor Bay, as the Dutch fleet had done unopposed when King William III came to claim the throne in 1688

This reprint 2007
First published 2001 by Bossiney Books,
Langore, Launceston, Cornwall PL15 8LD

ISBN 978-1899383-44-3

Acknowledgements
The photographs are reproduced by kind permission as follows:
Kent's Cavern, page 32; Roy Westlake, pages 13, 14, 28 and 29.
All other photographs are by Paul White.

The author is deeply grateful to Mr Leslie Retallick, Curator of Torre Abbey, for his advice and comments. Nevertheless any factual errors are entirely the responsibility of the author.

Printed in Great Britain by R Booth (Troutbeck Press), Mabe, Cornwall

Introduction

Modern Torbay is a 'conurbation' consisting of the three towns on Tor Bay (Torquay, Paignton and Brixham) and a number of villages, most of them absorbed in a continuous built-up area. Its story in the last two hundred years has been one of prosperity and growth, and growth tends to destroy or conceal what went before.

But if you know what to look for you can still find historical evidence of old roads, field and estate boundaries, the occasional old building and revealing place or street names. This book does not pretend to be a history of Torbay – it is far too short for that. But it will give you a general outline of the history of the towns, and, if you so choose, a framework for your own explorations on the ground and using maps and street plans. As a start, you may wish to compare the maps on pages 4 and 5 with a current 1:50,000 map.

The key to Torbay's history is its situation. Tor Bay is sheltered by Berry Head from the prevailing south-westerly winds. In the days of sail it was the best refuge in the Channel from the most destructive Atlantic gales. As such it was used by ships of all nations, and of none – pirates and privateers were not unknown and in the 17th century North African ships came hunting slaves from Devon.

The bay and its facilities became vital to the Navy in the endless wars with France during the 18th and early 19th centuries. Brixham in particular developed simultaneously as a fishing port and as an emergency source of fresh water and supplies.

Torquay on the other hand was developed firstly as a 'watering place' for invalids. It has a wonderful microclimate, with an enviable amount of sunshine, and faces south so can take full advantage. But its fastest growth came in the Victorian era when it became internationally fashionable as a winter resort for royalty and the very rich, and later used that reputation to attract the middle classes.

Paignton had been a substantial farming village since the middle ages, with a holiday home for the Bishops of Exeter. Its development as a resort began with the arrival of the railway in 1859. It targeted, then as now, summer visitors coming for a family holiday.

Benjamin Donn's one inch to the mile map of 1765

4

The Ordnance Survey map of 1929, 'with minor corrections to 1946'

The fish market in Brixham at the beginning of the 21st century

Brixham, the 'Mother of Trawling'

As is clear from the map on page 4, Brixham in 1765 consisted of two separate communities: Upper Brixham was a sizeable agricultural village (disparagingly referred to by the fishermen as 'up Cowtown') whilst the fishing village of Lower Brixham was a single street leading to the creek. At that time there was no real harbour, just quay walls to either side and a beach at The Strand, where the Tourist Information Office now is. The multi-storey car-park stands over what was once a tidal creek.

In the late eighteenth century a consortium of local families bought the harbour and acquired the delightful title of 'Quay Lords and Ladies'. They set about extending it in 1795 and began building the breakwater in 1800. It is surely no coincidence that this occurred when the Navy was using Brixham intensively as a supply depot, and the fishing industry was exploiting new grounds in the North Sea.

Over the centuries there have been many changes in where Brixham men have fished, which fish they have sought, and in their methods of fishing. Around 1750 a new kind of trawling grew up, possibly introduced by Beer fishermen who used Brixham rather than their own exposed beach. The 'beam' which held open the trawl net was made substantially longer, up to 15 metres, and the boats were built larger in order to handle the increased net size.

By the 1780s, fishermen from Brixham had begun trawling in the North Sea, finding and developing new fishing grounds and landing their fish at Grimsby and Hull. In consequence the fish markets in these places grew rapidly. By 1850 Brixham had 200 trawlers, most of them using distant ports to land their catches. All these boats were sail-powered and when steam trawlers were introduced to the North Sea the Brixham men responded by moving to new western fishing grounds rather than by converting to steam themselves.

Navigation in those days was done without even a chart. Just by bringing up a sample of the sea floor, experienced hands knew whereabouts they were. It was (and still is) a life of terrible danger, which created a close-knit working community, with the young men at sea and their families and the older men ashore, processing the catches and making equipment. There were several shipyards, building both trawlers and trading schooners.

Visitors will find that Brixham is still very much a working port where the rest of us are tolerated – and all the more interesting for it!

Whilst most of the surrounding houses are not particularly ancient, the general effect of the harbour is one of picturesque charm

This statue of William of Orange was erected in 1888. He reigned jointly with his wife Mary as William III (1688-1702). The landing of William of Orange was an event of major significance in British and Irish history.

Although he arrived at Brixham almost by chance, as a result of a fluke of the wind, his successful invasion concentrated everyone's minds on the strategic significance of Tor Bay

The landing at Brixham of William of Orange, 1688

The 'Glorious Revolution' of 1688 was a key point in British history, as it established a constitutional monarchy. The Stuart kings all had ambitions to absolute monarchy, and the last of them, James II, was openly a Catholic: he seemed to wish to reimpose Catholicism on his mainly Protestant people, which was a serious problem at that time. His Dutch son-in-law William of Orange was invited to take the thrones of England and Scotland – and of course to rule Ireland, where his Battle of the Boyne is remembered all too well.

'Parliament House'

It was late autumn when William set out from the Netherlands with an invasion fleet. Gales meant it was a matter of chance whether the fleet would be scattered. In the event, the fleet overshot Tor Bay and only an abrupt change of wind direction brought them back, at the same time halting James's fleet in its tracks by the Isle of Wight. William had three uninterrupted days to land 15,000 men, many of them British, together with horses and supplies.

His banner promised he would maintain 'the liberties of England and the Protestant Religion'. He was, tradition says, carried ashore by a fisherman named Varwell in whose house (since demolished) he spent his first night ashore. It is claimed that he said 'Mine goot people, I am come for your goots, for all your goots.' Well, maybe!

William's route was from Galmpton, through Waddeton, north of Stoke Gabriel, through Aish and towards Berry Pomeroy. And it can still be followed on the ground, being a most attractive Devon lane. He is said to have held his first Council meeting at Parliament House, and perhaps stayed the night there. Meanwhile his army headed for Newton Abbot, following the line of the present ring road to Marldon, then past Compton Castle to Abbotskerswell, on their way spending a very wet night in the muddy red fields.

Tor Bay and the Navy

Ex-King James took refuge in France, where Louis XIV supported him half-heartedly in his attempts to regain the throne.

War with France, or the prospect of such a war, was the normal state of affairs from 1688 to 1815. The key to these wars was trade: whichever country could control their enemy's trade would effectively be winning the war.

France's main naval port in the north was Brest. William immediately developed Plymouth as a naval dockyard but Plymouth Sound was a poor anchorage – captains complained their ships bumped on the bottom in any swell! – and Tor Bay was often preferred. From the 1760s, English strategy in wartime was to blockade Brest. Whenever there was a westerly gale off Ushant (which was often) the English fleet ran for cover to Tor Bay, knowing that the French could not leave port. But as soon as the wind changed, they had to rush back to their blockading station.

Their visits to Tor Bay in wartime had the character of pit-stops. Those ashore saw them coming, sometimes to Plymouth, sometimes Tor Bay, and tried to gather together adequate supplies of meat, bread and beer (considered vital as a protection against scurvy) and get them to the appropriate place.

The fleet contained some 25,000 men, a population about the same size as Plymouth's. This put enormous strains on the local people: prices went sky high and while farmers, merchants and

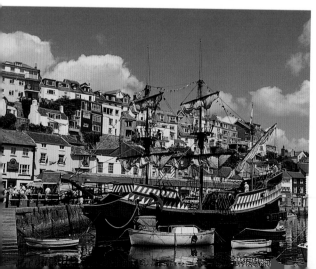

Left: a replica of the Golden Hind *helps attract tourists to Brixham Harbour*

Opposite: many visitors are perfectly happy with the modern realities of a working harbour

brewers were making fortunes, the poor were often starving. There were a number of food riots as a result.

The fleet's visits were so frequent that some officers' families began to take lodgings in the Tor Bay area to await them. It used to be said that this was the beginning of Torquay's development, but that probably exaggerates the numbers involved.

When the wars finally ended, after the Battle of Waterloo, Napoleon surrendered to the British and was brought to Tor Bay on 24 July 1815 aboard the 74-gun *Bellerophon*. He remarked 'Enfin, voilà ce beau pays.' (Well, he was a soldier, not a poet!) During the 48 hours he remained in Tor Bay, hundreds of boats brought curious sightseers to see the man who had dominated the world. He found the attention gratifying, but was soon bundled off to remote St Helena, where he would die – possibly poisoned by a British agent.

Tor Bay's usefulness to the Navy declined in the 19th century as Plymouth was developed and the days of sail came to end. But in 1944 the Torbay harbours were intensively used for the Normandy landings: a number of slipways built at that time are still in use.

Remains of the fourteenth century Bishop's Palace at Paignton

Paignton

If the Walrus and the Carpenter had been walking at Paignton, 'talking of many things', they would have discussed cabbages and bishops rather than cabbages and kings. Paignton (or Paington as it was more commonly spelled and perhaps pronounced in 1800) was famous for its cabbages! In those days before uniform seed lists and national seed-merchants, local varieties of vegetables could be very significant. Hundreds of cartloads of Paignton's 'flatpolls' and a variety of spring cabbage were exported along the coast from Land's End to London, and even, it has been claimed, to Newfoundland.

The bishops of Exeter had acquired the manor of Paignton before the Norman Conquest, but the settlement may already have existed by AD 700. It was a thriving agricultural community and included vineyards and salt pans (salt played a vital part in the medieval economy) as well as fields and grazing lands. In Saxon times the manor also included a substantial part of southern Dartmoor, probably used for summer grazing.

Just as in driving through Paignton you might never realise it has surviving medieval buildings, so you could fail to find its harbour, tucked under Roundham Head. Yet there was a fishing harbour and fish market here by 1567, and probably centuries earlier

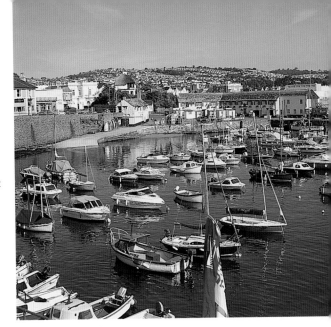

Visitors could be forgiven for never finding the historic aspects of Paignton: they are not particularly remarkable, but well worth the effort of hunting them out. The core of the old village was inland from the present centre. It was based on modern Winner Street and Church Street, where a few old buildings survive, as well as the large red sandstone church itself, noted for its Kirkham Chantry.

Immediately across the road from the church is a flight of steps leading into a modern housing development. Bear right through this and you'll come to the Old Clink – a 'lock-up' the size of a woodshed, of a kind which every small town possessed, with the same function as modern police cells. Beyond the Clink you'll come to Littlegate Road: turn left and in a few metres reach the medieval Kirkham House, probably the home of a chantry priest. Unfortunately it has limited opening hours.

The area south of the church was occupied by the Palace, of which only the external fortifications remain. These were just about adequate to protect the building against French raiding parties. Another street with older houses is Old Torquay Road, north of Oldway Mansion (built by Isaac Singer of sewing machine fame).

The Paignton & Dartmouth Railway actually runs to Kingswear; it is mostly steam-hauled and connects with a ferry to Dartmouth

The railway

The arrival of the railway in Paignton in 1859 spurred a great growth in the town, as entrepreneurs such as Mr R Fletcher of Birmingham bought up land between the railway and the sea and rapidly began to develop it. The extensive dunes were turned into public gardens, the pier was opened in 1879, and bandstands and a public theatre soon followed. (This apparently staged the world premiere of *The Pirates of Penzance* in December 1879.)

The South Devon Railway had reached Torquay in 1848, but only as far as what is now Torre Station. They had planned to use Brunel's new atmospheric system. It was a brilliant idea but the technology of the time was not adequate, so it was a complete financial disaster. Brunel shrugged his shoulders and marched on, but the South Devon Railway never fully recovered. A new company, the Dartmouth &

Torbay, was formed to take the line to what is now Torquay station. The town of Torquay wanted a more central site but the Cary family at Torre Abbey would not allow the railway on their land. This line was extended to Paignton in 1859, then to 'Brixham Road' and Kingswear. The aim was a viaduct across the Dart and ultimately a line all the way to Plymouth, but the owner of Greenway House near Galmpton (later owned by Agatha Christie) scuppered the plan and a terminus at Kingswear was the best they could do.

It was normal to celebrate the arrival of a new railway with great civic celebrations and gifts of food to the poor. At Paignton they baked a traditional 'Paignton Pudding'. It weighed $1^1/_2$ tonnes and needed six horses to pull it. There were 18,000 people present, most of them uninvited. A local historian wrote:

> The mob literally swarmed around the wagon, and mounting the wheels, proceeded to demolish the pudding; alarmed at the menacing attitude of the crowd, the Committee threw the pudding piecemeal among them. A disgraceful scene followed in which men, women and boys struggled and fought for possession of the pieces thrown out from the waggon, and this continued until not a morsel was left... For weeks afterwards the Post Office was inundated with greasy packets containing morsels of the pudding sent off as souvenirs to distant friends.

Paignton Pier, opened in 1879 and still at the heart of the traditional seaside holiday experience in which the town excels

Torquay harbour then and now

The lithograph above dates from about 1835, the photograph opposite from 2000. Given the pace of change in Torquay, it is perhaps surprising how much had *not* altered! Most of the buildings in the print had been erected since 1800 and are still there – including the Italianate Rock House on Waldon Hill, with its red shutters.

In 1835 the harbour was a hive of commercial activity: where a two-master is moored against a quay, there was a coal wharf and sheds (played down by the artist). Fleet Street, the heart of Torquay, scarcely exists. Instead we have a beautiful green valley. The scenery must have been unbelievably attractive before development began, and indeed that is what enticed the earliest visitors such as the Rev. Swete, who found it picturesque in the extreme. But he also thought it capable of development into a resort 'of unparalleled beauty'.

Perhaps the greatest difference between the print and the photograph is the total absence in 1835 of any road or even foreshore under Waldon Hill, or along the Torre Abbey Sands.

How Torquay developed

The valley which contains Union Street belongs to the Fleet brook, which now flows underground. To the left of the valley, looking from the harbour, and hidden behind the hill, is Torre (once known as Tor Mohun, after the Norman family which had owned it).

Some time in the Middle Ages Torre apparently acquired a fishing outpost on the waterfront, 'Tor Key'. The manor of Torre was owned by Torre Abbey when the monasteries were dissolved in 1539.

By 1662 Torre Abbey, Torre village and most of the land to the west of the Fleet brook (on the left from this viewpoint) were in the hands of the Carys, an old 'County' family. To the east of the Fleet valley had by that time become a separate manor, Torwood. This was owned until 1768 by the Ridgeway family, Earls of Londonderry. There seems to have been some antagonism between the two estates even before the Ridgeways sold out to Robert Palk, the son of an Ashburton farmer, a self-made man with a huge fortune.

Torquay sprang from the creative tension which followed!

Torre Abbey around 1800, when Admiral Lord Nelson was a visitor

Torre Abbey

The abbey was founded by William de Brewer, one of Richard the Lionheart's close supporters, in 1196-98. The abbot and canons would – at least in later years – have lived well, especially the abbot. At the Dissolution, the then Abbot took a pension of £64 p.a. whilst the 15 canons received £62 p.a. between them.

Various parts of the Abbey's possessions changed hands several times but in 1662 Torre Abbey and Torre were bought by the Cary family who had held Cockington from 1373 until they lost it through supporting King Charles I in the Civil War. The Carys were staunch Catholics, conservative landowners and without social rivals locally.

The present house (open to the public for much of the year) was adapted from the abbey remains in the 18th century, so it has a Georgian front facing the sea and a largely medieval west side, including the Mohun Gateway of c.1320. It was bought by the Corporation in 1930 for a mere £40,000. The grounds extended without interruption to the beach, and were subject to erosion by the sea.

The 'Spanish Barn' of Torre Abbey

This beautiful tithe barn belonged to the abbey, and may well date back to 1200. It gets the name 'Spanish' from a sad incident in 1588 during the battle with the Armada. One of the Spanish galleons, *Nostra Señora del Rosario*, was seriously damaged by a collision. The next morning she was taken by Sir Francis Drake. (He had deserted his leading place in the line of battle entirely for his own personal profit, but he was too popular to court-martial!)

There were 397 prisoners, no standard way of dealing with them, and certainly no equivalent of the Geneva Convention. Many Devon sailors had suffered in Spanish prisons and had had friends killed by the Inquisition. There were national and religious animosities long before this Spanish attempt to invade England.

Sir George Cary had the prisoners locked in the barn, leaving the then owner a large barrel of wine in recompense. Details are sketchy. A week later, 211 were marched to Exeter and 166 were returned to their ship. Provisioning was distinctly hit or miss, and it seems likely that at least some of the prisoners died.

The former parish church of Torre

Many visitors to Torquay probably miss the 'urban village' of Torre, which occupies the top end of Union Street. Sandwiched between this and a similar 'village' at the top of Belgrave Road lies the heart of old Torre, where it has existed since before the Norman Conquest. It is of course totally built over, but well worth exploring on foot.

The ancient parish church, St Saviour's, was heavily restored in Victorian times. Many larger churches were also built to accommodate the wealthy visitors who flocked into the town. In the 1980s St Saviour's became a Greek Orthodox church.

Torre (or Tor or Tor Mohun) gets its name from an actual tor – a great crag between Tor Hill Road and St Efride's Road, so built onto, over, and into, that today you have to actively look for it. But it must have been a major landmark from the sea in earlier times.

One other medieval chapel survives, St Michael's chapel, a very simple building high on a rock just north of Torre Station. You can approach it by a surprisingly lonely footpath from Briwere Road.

'Fleete, otherwise Tor Key'

The map on page 4 hints at just a few buildings around the harbour, without a single road leading to them. Mostly they were fishermen's cottages but five were small ale-houses and there was one 'respectable' inn. Just inland was a mill – where the roundabout is now at the top of Fleet Street – which was 'picturesque' on account of being partly in ruins. This hamlet itself was sometimes known as 'Fleet'.

A vogue for sea bathing had started in the 1730s, and by the late 18th century Exmouth, Dawlish and Teignmouth had already developed as fashionable resorts: Torquay had the setting to compete, but was virtually inaccessible by land.

About 1790 a humble row of cottages for visitors, just below the cliff on what is now Cary Parade, started a new trend. In 1794 a visitor wrote that 'instead of the poor uncomfortable village we had imagined, we saw a pretty range of neat new buildings fitted out for summer visitors, who very certainly enjoy convenient bathing, retirement and a most romantic situation.'

The first development in modern Torquay was what later became Cary Parade. A Mr Searle, joiner and architect, had the cliff cut back and built a row of cottages for the accommodation of visitors.

The buildings behind Golden Palms are probably part of that first speculation. The red shutters belong to Rock House

Palks and Carys

Robert Palk was born in 1717, son of a farmer. He went to Oxford as a 'sizar' (a student who worked his way by acting as a servant to the richer students), became a naval chaplain, stopped off in India, became indispensable to the East India Company administrators as a diplomat, and ultimately became Governor of Madras. His abilities as a merchant, as well as the inevitable 'gifts' which came his way, meant that he retired to Devon a very rich man, and he bought Torwood Grange with a view to living as a country gentleman.

George Cary of Torre Abbey could not consider a farmer's son a gentleman. Squabbles and litigation ensued. As it happened, the fields directly opposite Torwood Grange and a rocky outcrop (on which the Torquay Museum now stands) were owned by Cary. Palk was uneasily aware that at any moment Cary could build an eyesore to affront his view! So instead of settling at Torwood, he bought an enormous mansion, Haldon House in Dunchideock.

Whilst the very first development (Searle's cottages) had been on Cary land, it was the Palk lands which were most rapidly developed, because the Palks saw them more as an investment than as a home. The Carys were left fighting not-in-my-back-yard actions – until in time they opted to join in the development fun and games.

Sir Lawrence Palk at first concentrated on developing the harbour; the inner harbour was completed in 1806. He rented out the whole of Waldon Hill for a mere £15 p.a. and everything from the Quay to Daddy Hole Plain for £40 p.a. He seems to have mismanaged his finances before dying in 1813. The estate was then most energetically managed for the Palks by a Dr Henry Beeke, a Kingsteignton man with an impressive academic and clerical career already behind him. But it was William Kitson, the Palk Estate manager from 1833 to 1874, who in effect created Torquay. A contemporary wrote:

> The hills, hitherto inaccessible, were opened up by roads which were planned by him; the symmetrical arrangement of the villas on the sloping hills were the result of his fertile ingenuity.

Torquay's rapid development and great prosperity during the nineteenth century has left it with a wealth of nineteenth century architecture. The earliest examples are in the late Georgian style (top). 'The Terrace' itself was started in 1810.

The middle photograph shows a style of villa which became popular in Torquay, with a light verandah on three sides. Most date from the 1820s and 1830s.

As the Victorian period proceeded, buildings became more solid and details became heavier. Rounded arches over doorways and square Italianate towers typify the mid-Victorian period. This example dates from the 1850s

23

Hesketh Crescent, 1849, included a hotel and ten large houses for rent

Kitson was also responsible for creating a waterworks, gas lighting, markets, drainage and local government bodies. He added a bank to his personal portfolio, and he himself had a substantial stake in the success of the town and its inhabitants. Meanwhile the Palks continued acting out the old adage 'rags to rags in three generations' except that it was not till the death of the fourth baronet that their fortunes, heavily mortgaged and overspent, collapsed totally in 1883.

Torquay was a late starter among Devon holiday resorts but it aimed high. In the eighteenth century rich English people overwintered at Montpellier in the south of France, in the twentieth century it would be Monte Carlo – but in Victorian times European royalty and the 'upper crust' headed for Torquay in winter. Victoria and Albert made several visits by yacht. The town preened!

But fashions change and the jet set acquired its jets and moved on long ago. Genteel Torquay has (not without opposition from retired residents) adjusted its sights to a much wider variety of visitors.

Above: Lisburne Terrace, built in 1851. The Palk Estate under William Kitson was instrumental in getting superb holiday homes built for wealthy visitors, but what they failed to do was create the necessary homes for the humbler people who were vital to the smooth running of the town.

An undercurrent in Torquay's history, for which there is no space in this little book, involves working class discontent, which led to several 'bread riots'

Below: overlooking Torre Church are these monumental ruins, like something out of ancient Rome! On top were the gardens of Lauriston Hall, a Victorian mansion bombed in the war. By retreating to the back of the gardens, the owners could avoid the frequent sight of burials in the church yard

The rather sad little Victorian building below the cliff, easily mistaken for a disused public convenience, actually represents a key moment in Torbay's history. This is the Toll House on the Torbay Road, newly opened in 1842.

For the first time it was possible to go round the foot of the cliffs. Until that moment Torquay was confined to the harbour. Suddenly the Abbey sands were accessible and the walk to Cockington became a vital part of the holiday experience!

A question of accessibility

A look at Donn's map (page 4) will show how isolated Torquay was in 1765. Such 'roads' as there were were scarcely passable by wheeled vehicles. A friend suggested to Sir LV Palk that his developments would never thrive until people could reach the town easily by land.

In one day, they staked out the line of a new road from Union Street along a very narrow strip of Palk land past Chapel Hill and on to Kingskerswell – still broadly the main access today, though much improved since Palk's time. When Shaldon Bridge was opened in 1827, the road from there to Torquay was improved and widened.

These works were carried out by the Turnpike Trustees – but Palk's man Kitson was the guiding force. In 1842 they blasted a road under Waldon Hill and – despite protests – across the Cary lands at Torre Abbey. This involved sea defences which have always been hard to maintain against severe easterly gales. The 'Torbay Road' was then extended to Paignton, where it radically changed the focus of the town away from Winner Street, and on to the fish quay at Brixham.

Cockington Court, former home of the Mallock family

Cockington

There is something very odd about Cockington. It presents itself as a historic village, but to anyone used to historic English villages it looks highly artificial – a place for cream and twee. In addition to chocolate box thatched cottages there is a pub designed by the great imperial architect Lutyens and a 'picturesque' gatekeeper's lodge of 1839. What *is* going on?

The Rev. Roger Mallock inherited the ancient manor of Cockington in 1786 and for the next 60 years he was both its squire and its parson. The village in 1786 was clustered around the church. The new 'squarson' immediately started modernising his house, creating the pleasant if uninspiring building which survives.

Then he looked out from his new doorway and didn't like what he saw – poor people and their nasty dwellings. So he had the barns and cottages knocked down and rebuilt the village out of sight, but in 'picturesque' style. The Cockington theme park was created in 1810!

Cockington Church: the squarson obliterated the graveyard

It is easy to feel indignant about such proceedings, which were not that unusual in England at that time. The Rev. Mallock certainly never consulted the people whose lives he disrupted, but it is at least possible that in some cases they were better housed than before.

After his death in 1846, later Mallocks had to face the invasion of their idyllic rural stronghold by tourists, extension of the railway to Livermead (Torquay Station) over their lands, and a massive growth of housing in the once delightful village of Chelston, another manor which they owned. They profited, but R H Mallock found he could not protect his privacy and Torquay bought Cockington in 1932.

Quintessential Cockington – interesting, yet not quite what it seems

Right: this is 'Old Paignton Road', now a footpath. It was still in 1765 the main road from Paignton through Cockington to Torre (see the map on page 4). If you park in Broadley Drive, you can walk down to the village, using these ancient sandstone steps (slippery after rain). They formed the middle of what is probably the medieval road surface, with a rut either side created by sledges – wheeled vehicles being unknown before about 1750.

Many other routes on Donn's map can still be traced as twisting lanes amid the suburbs of Torbay

Marldon

Marldon lies at the centre of the ancient road network of Torbay and must have been one of the larger settlements in medieval times. Just outside the ring-road, it has managed to preserve a village character. The church is mainly 15th century, and so is the Church House pub, hard though it is to believe it given the bizarre 'Gothick' windows.

Church houses are common in Devon: most of them were built in the 15th century and they served the community on Sunday, providing refreshments and a place to go between services. Men and women occupied separate floors. They were also the venue for parish festivities such as feast days and church ales, and their survival as the village pub is a natural extension of that old convivial role.

Another village now part of Torbay is St Marychurch which, with its hamlet of Babbacombe, was incorporated into Torquay against its will in 1900. If they are omitted from this book, it is out of respect for their independent history – as well as shortage of space!

Compton Castle

Compton Castle is a fortified manor house, originally dating from the 14th century. Much of what we can now see, including the fortification, dates from the early 16th century, when first French and later Spanish raids on the south coast were frequent. It was not designed to withstand a determined siege.

Whilst the castle is fascinating to visit, you need to plan around its somewhat restricted opening hours. It is owned by The National Trust but occupied and administered by Mr and Mrs Gilbert, whose family has lived there for most of the last 600 years. Sir Humphrey Gilbert and two successive Sir John Gilberts were noted Elizabethan sailors, and the family was deeply involved in the colonisation of North America. Sir Walter Ralegh was a close relation.

Sir Humphrey Gilbert was responsible for founding one of England's first colonies, claiming possession of the island of Newfoundland on 3 August 1583. He died on the return journey. Sir Humphrey's charter from Queen Elizabeth to search for any lands not already in possession of a Christian monarch passed to Sir Walter Ralegh, his half-brother, who founded a colony on Roanoke Island, Virginia, but it did not survive.

Kent's Cavern

Neanderthal people used Kent's Cavern at least 350,000 years ago and it was clearly used by hunting parties of our own species during the Ice Ages. As such, it is really part of pre-history and might be thought out of place in a book on Torbay's visible history.

Actually it occupies a very significant place in intellectual history. It was in his excavations here, and at another cave in Brixham, that local scientist William Pengelly effectively invented our modern archaeological techniques of recording, in which every object found is meticulously located in a three-dimensional grid. In so doing, Pengelly helped prove scientifically that mankind had been on earth much longer than was suggested by the Bible.

As a limestone cave, the Cavern is attractive in its own right, but its record of human habitation and its significance to science and archaeology add greatly to its interest. The natural sequel is to visit the excellent Torquay Museum, of which Pengelly was a founder.